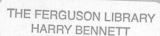

W9-CCO-347

A DREAM OF FLIGHT

ALBERTO SANTOS-DUMONT'S RACE AROUND THE EIFFEL TOWER

ROB POLIVKA AND **JEF POLIVKA**

ILLUSTRATIONS BY **ROB POLIVKA**

Farrar Straus Giroux
New York

For Jenna. I want to go where you go and be where you be. —R. P.
For Emily, the propeller on my balloon. —J. P.

Farrar Straus Giroux Books for Young Readers
An imprint of Macmillan Publishing Group, LLC

120 Broadway, New York, NY 10271
Copyright © 2019 by Rob Polivka and Jef Polivka
All rights reserved
Color separations by Embassy Graphics
Printed in China by RR Donnelley Asia Printing Solutions Ltd.,
Dongguan City, Guangdong Province
Designed by Monique Sterling
First edition, 2019

1 3 5 7 9 10 8 6 4 2

mackids.com

Page 39: Photo of Alberto Santos-Dumont by Nélson Freire Lavanére-Wanderley, 1916 © Alamy Stock Photo

Library of Congress Cataloging-in-Publication Data

Names: Polivka, Rob, author. | Polivka-Searle, Jef, author.
Title: A dream of flight : Alberto Santos-Dumont's race around the Eiffel Tower /
Rob Polivka and Jef Polivka-Searle ;
  Illustrations by Rob Polivka.
Description: First edition. | New York : Farrar Straus Giroux, 2019. |
  Audience: Age 4-8.
Identifiers: LCCN 2018035772 | ISBN 9780374306618 (hardcover)
Subjects: LCSH: Santos-Dumont, Alberto, 1873-1932—Biography—Juvenile
  literature. | Aeronautical engineers—Brazil—Biography—Juvenile
  literature. | Airships—History—Juvenile literature. | Balloon
  ascensions—History—Juvenile literature. | CYAC: Aeronautical engineers.
  | Airships. | Balloon ascensions.
Classification: LCC TL540.S25 P65 2019 | DDC 629.13092 [B] —dc23
LC record available at https://lccn.loc.gov/2018035772

Our books may be purchased in bulk for promotional, educational, or business use.
Please contact your local bookseller or the Macmillan Corporate and Premium Sales Department
at (800) 221-7945 ext. 5442 or by email at MacmillanSpecialMarkets@macmillan.com.

Long ago, before the invention of the airplane, a boy dreamed that one day, he would fly. The boy's name was Alberto Santos-Dumont. Santos for short.

Santos grew up in Brazil.

From a young age, he worked on his father's large coffee plantation.

He loved to help with the machines that harvested and transported the coffee. His favorite was the coffee sorter. The machine seemed to work by magic as it turned dirty, raw coffee cherries into clean and shiny beans. Santos was fascinated.

As Santos grew older, his interest in
machines grew, too. He wanted to learn
all he could about life and about the way
things work.

So when he became a young man, Santos left his home in Brazil to study science in France.

The journey, by steamship and train, took more than a week.

Santos arrived in Paris in the summer of 1892.

The city enchanted him. It was beautiful, rich in art and culture, and home to great marvels of technology and engineering.

The most famous of these marvels, the Eiffel Tower, rose high above the city, as if to remind Santos of the possibilities before him.

Santos experienced the best of Paris life. He made friends, and dined with them at fine restaurants and cafés.

And while most people still traveled by horse and carriage, Santos zoomed all over town in his little automobile.

He worked and studied, tinkered and tested, but never forgot his dream of flight.

One day, Santos decided to hire a
balloon maker to take him for a trip.
   The flight was not what Santos
had expected. The air was so
still, it seemed as if he was
standing in place and the ground
moved away under his feet.

It was a strange sensation, but a beautiful one.

The balloon climbed higher and higher until the world below vanished beneath an ocean of white puffs.

Santos thought this was the perfect time to break for lunch.

He unpacked roast beef, cheese, and fruit, with ice cream for dessert. Then he poured champagne, and he and the balloon maker drank a toast. In the chilly mist of the clouds, crystals of snow formed on their glasses and sparkled in the sunlight.

Santos and the balloon maker enjoyed the most exquisite meal of their lives as they dined above the clouds.

HYDROGEN BALLOON   AIRSHIP NO. 1

Santos was so inspired by his trip, he decided to design a balloon of his own. But he was not content to make one that merely floated, like the hydrogen balloon.

He would make a long, narrow one that could sail through the air like a ship through water.

To move by its own power, the balloon would need a motor. So Santos took the engine from his little car and affixed it to the balloon's basket. A propeller attached to the engine would push the airship through the sky.

He called it *Airship No. 1.*

When his friends heard about his plans, they feared for his safety.

"The hydrogen gas that fills your balloon is highly flammable! If your engine makes a spark, it will ignite the balloon, and your airship will crash in flames! Perhaps people are not meant to fly, Santos," they said.

But Santos had faith in his little engine.

"There will be no sparks," he said.

On September 18, 1898, *Airship No. 1* made its debut flight before a large crowd at Paris's botanical gardens. Santos's friends watched nervously as he prepared the airship. Everyone expected Santos to take off with the wind, as pilots of unpowered balloons did.

Santos protested. He wanted to begin his flight *into* the wind, because he knew his airship could move forward through it, unlike the unpowered balloons.

But the crowd insisted. With the wind and propeller pushing it along, *Airship No. 1* raced forward! Before it had time to rise high into the air, it crashed into the tall trees at the end of the field.

As Santos climbed down from the wreckage, he vowed to never again ignore his instincts.

Santos went back to the drawing board right away. Over the next few years, he designed and built more airships. Each design improved upon the one before it.

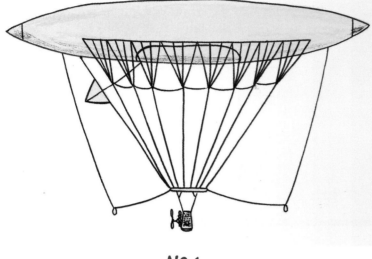

His first airship—or powered, steerable balloon—was shaped like a cylinder and was eighty-two feet long.

NO. 1

Santos built his airships of the highest-quality materials he could find. His balloons were made of fine, lightweight Japanese silk, and coated with varnish for extra strength.

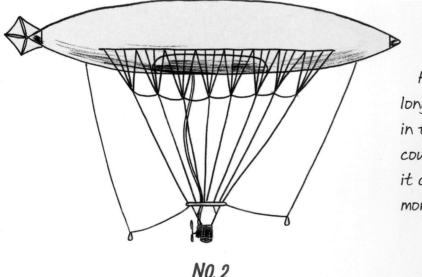

His second airship was as long as the first, but wider in the middle. The balloon could hold more hydrogen, so it could rise into the air more easily.

NO. 2

But these first two airships' balloons were so long, they had a bad habit of folding then collapsing in the middle if they lost pressure.

To solve this problem, Santos gave his next airship a shorter, wider balloon. It could hold even more gas than No. 2, and could move upward better than ever.

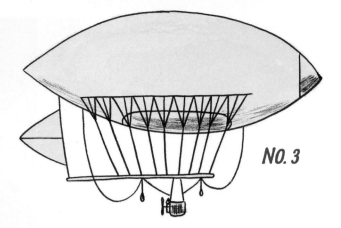

NO. 3

Santos made sure his airships were as light as possible. Instead of rope to attach the basket to the balloon, he used thin, strong piano wire. For the frames, he used pine or bamboo.

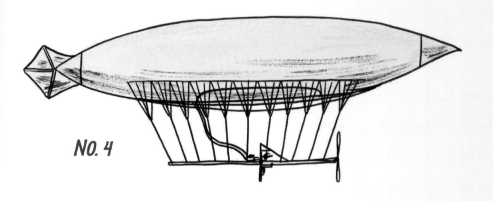

NO. 4

He did not even give Airship No. 4 a pilot's basket. Instead, a bicycle seat was fastened to a single bamboo pole.

By the time he built No. 5, Santos had found elegant solutions to many problems common in balloon flight.

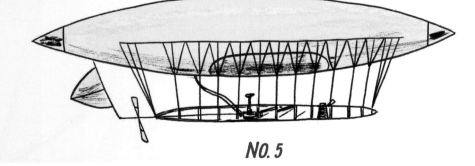

NO. 5

Other balloons had to throw off weight or let out gas to move higher or lower. Santos used a system of weights, which could be shifted forward or backward on ropes to point the nose of the balloon up or down.

The airship's propeller could then push it in any direction.

Almost every time he flew, something went wrong.

But Santos was never discouraged. He learned from each mistake, and always took to the air once more to try again. He knew that the power of flight could change the world, and so he pushed on.

People everywhere were in awe of Santos's daring adventures and inspired by dreams of flight.

Men copied his stylish Panama hats. Toy shops sold models of his airships, and bakeries even made little cookies in the shape of them.

Newspaper reporters followed him everywhere and wrote down what he did. They dubbed him "Le Petit Santos."

Because aviation was so new and exciting, the Aero Club was formed to encourage its progress. One day, a wealthy club member named Henri Deutsch made an announcement. He would award 100,000 francs to the first person who could pilot an airship from the club around the Eiffel Tower and back in thirty minutes or less.

Powered-balloon flights had been made before, but they had been limited and unpredictable. Most people still did not believe that sustained, controlled flight was possible.

This was the opportunity Santos had been waiting for! If he met Deutsch's challenge, he would prove to the world that people could really fly.

One morning, Santos was making good time as he raced for the Deutsch Prize. He circled the tower easily in nine minutes, which left plenty of time to return to the Aero Club . . .

. . . when disaster struck! A pressure valve inside the balloon began to leak. If the balloon lost its shape, it could stress the airship's wires and snap them, sending Santos and his little basket to the ground.

The partially deflated balloon rocked up and down like a seesaw. Santos hoped he could land in the nearby river Seine, but just before the river stood a large hotel.

Another attempt had failed. Santos was not hurt, but this was the end of *Airship No. 5*.

Despite the crash, Santos did not become discouraged. Each time he went back to his workshop to repair his airship, he knew he was one step closer to winning the prize.

The victory would not belong to him alone. Santos promised to give away the prize money if he should win: half to the workers who helped him build his airships, and half to the poor people of Paris.

Indeed, Santos believed that the whole world would benefit if he succeeded.

He hoped that by allowing people to visit other lands, flight would bring cultures together and show everyone how alike they are at heart.

On October 19, 1901, an enormous crowd gathered to watch Santos and his splendid *Airship No. 6* ascend from the Aero Club grounds and head for the Eiffel Tower.

Santos would race alone, against the clock, to show that real, controlled flight was possible.

This time, everyone felt sure he would win the Deutsch Prize.

Despite a strong wind blowing against the side of the ship, *No. 6* reached the tower without incident. Everyone cheered for Santos as he circled the tower and steered his airship back toward the Aero Club.

Just as *No. 6* entered the home stretch, its motor began to sputter and stop. Santos was forced to leave his basket and tend to the engine.

Santos balanced on the wooden frame as he made his way to the engine. People below watched his tiny figure, fearing the fate Santos had so narrowly avoided not long before would certainly befall him today.

But Santos had no time for fear.

He adjusted the engine and quickly returned to the basket. But the airship had lost so much altitude that Santos had to act swiftly.

He pointed the airship's nose to the sky. The power of the propeller pushed it upward, and Santos was saved from disaster.

No. 6 approached the finish line at last. The question still remained: Would he make it in time?

As he neared the ground, Santos could hear the cheers of the crowd below. He called out, "Have I won?"

"Yes, you have done it, Santos!" the crowd roared.

Airship No. 6 had crossed the finish line at twenty-nine minutes and thirty seconds. He had done it at last!

Santos had played his part in the world's dream of flight. That dream, elusive for centuries, was finally beginning to come true. Soon, people all over the world would visit distant lands.

They would connect
with unfamiliar cultures.
And they would feel the
thrill, unlike any other, of
rising above the clouds.

Soon, like birds,
they would fly.

Alberto Santos-Dumont (1916)
Photograph by Nélson Freire Lavanére-Wanderley

AUTHORS' NOTE

For most of human history, flight seemed a romantic and impossible dream. This book is a chapter in the life of a boy from Brazil who grew up to realize that dream and became the toast of Paris. His brilliance, his ingenuity, and his contributions to aviation, carried out with such style, made him an irresistible subject.

BIBLIOGRAPHY

Man Flies: The Story of Alberto Santos-Dumont, Master of the Balloon, Conquerer of the Air by Nancy Winters (Bloomsbury, 1997)

My Airships by Alberto Santos-Dumont (Grant Richards, 1904)

Wings of Madness by Paul Hoffman (Hachette, 2003)

FUN FACTS ABOUT ALBERTO SANTOS-DUMONT

· Throughout his life, Santos was proud to hold no patents on his flying machines. He made his designs available to all, as he hoped that flight would unite the world in peace.

· Though he was shy, Santos delighted people with his eccentricities. He invited friends to dine with him "on the ceiling." In his apartment, he had a table and chairs built so high off the ground that guests had to reach their seats by stepladder!

· Santos signed his name with an equal sign (Santos=Dumont) to give equality to both parts of his surname.

· He enlisted his friend Louis Cartier to design a timepiece that would allow him to time his flights without removing his hands from his airship's controls. The result led to the rise in popularity of the wristwatch over the pocket watch. Cartier then named the watch after his friend.

A BRIEF TIMELINE OF AERONAUTICS INVENTION AND ALBERTO SANTOS-DUMONT

1783 Joseph and Étienne Montgolfier invent the hot-air balloon. Then Jacques César Charles adapts the Montgolfier brothers' design and invents the hydrogen balloon.

1852 Henri Giffard invents a self-propelled, steam-powered balloon.

1873 Alberto Santos-Dumont is born in Minas Gerais, Brazil.

1891 Santos's father, Henrique, becomes ill and takes the family with him to Europe in search of treatment. Santos becomes enchanted with Paris, and moves there permanently the following year.

1897 Santos reads an account of a balloon expedition to the North Pole written by Parisians Henri Lachambre and Alexis Machuron. This book convinces Santos to pursue ballooning. Later this year, Santos designs his first balloon, named *Brazil*, which is built with the help of Lachambre and Machuron.

1898 Santos designs and flies his first steerable balloon, the *Airship Santos-Dumont No. 1*.

1901 Santos wins the Deutsch Prize with *Airship No. 6*.

1902 Santos flies *Airship No. 6* in Monaco. The airship deflates and crashes into the Mediterranean Sea. Later, Santos brings *Airship No. 7* to the United States and meets Thomas Edison and Theodore Roosevelt. Santos then designs *No. 9*—an airship so small, he can park it outside his apartment on the streets of Paris.

1903 Wilbur and Orville Wright invent the first airplane capable of sustained, controlled flight.

1906 Santos designs his first airplane, named *No. 14-bis* ("14-encore"), and makes the first heavier-than-air flight in Europe.

1909 Santos designs another airplane, *No. 20*, nicknamed Demoiselle, or "dragonfly." He flies this elegant little plane as freely as if it were a personal flying car. This becomes the precursor to the modern ultralight airplane. Louis Blériot also crosses the English Channel in an airplane this year.

1927 Charles Lindbergh flies an airplane across the Atlantic Ocean.

1932 Amelia Earhart is the first woman to pilot an airplane across the Atlantic. A few months later, in July, Alberto Santos-Dumont dies in Brazil.